Original title:
Radiant Embrace

Copyright © 2024 Swan Charm
All rights reserved.

Author: Kene Elistrand
ISBN HARDBACK: 978-9908-1-2746-0
ISBN PAPERBACK: 978-9908-1-2747-7
ISBN EBOOK: 978-9908-1-2748-4

Lightwoven Souls

In twilight's embrace, they begin to glow,
Threads of connection, in whispers they flow.
Bright flickers of laughter, like stars in the night,
Each heartbeat a promise, in soft silver light.

Together they wander, through shadows and dreams,
Weaving their stories, or so it seems.
With each step they take, their spirits entwine,
Bound by the magic, of love so divine.

Dance of Sunlit Hearts

In morning's light, they sway and twirl,
Sunlit laughter, as bright as a pearl.
Every movement paints, a story untold,
In the warmth of the sun, their dreams unfold.

With every beat, the world fades away,
Lost in the rhythm, where shadows can't stay.
Together they dance, as the sky turns blue,
Hearts interlocked, in a waltz ever true.

The Elegance of Gentle Touches

Fingers glide softly, like whispers in air,
Each touch a promise, gentle and rare.
Moments of silence, where feelings ignite,
In the hush of the night, everything feels right.

A brush of the hand, a glance full of grace,
Time stands still in this sacred space.
With every connection, they silently speak,
In the power of touch, their souls intertwine, unique.

Radiance in Every Breath

Inhale the beauty, exhale the pain,
Every breath taken, a moment to gain.
Sparkles of joy, in rhythm they rise,
Painting the world with wonder and skies.

With each rising sun, a chance to renew,
Finding the magic in all that they do.
In every heartbeat, a story unfolds,
Radiant whispers of truths to be told.

Light's Tender Ricochet

In quiet dusk, the colors blend,
Soft whispers dance, as shadows mend.
A spark ignites in evening's glow,
Reflecting dreams we both can sow.

Each glimmer shines, a gentle tease,
Through tangled paths, our hearts find ease.
The world transforms, the night takes flight,
In every beam, our hopes unite.

The Warm Glow of Companionship

With every laugh, a light we share,
In cozy nooks, we find our air.
A gaze that warms, a touch that heals,
In silent bonds, our spirit feels.

Through storms we stand, our courage bold,
In stories rich, our lives unfold.
Together we shine, a beacon bright,
In friendship's glow, we own the night.

Fractals of Joyful Togetherness

In moments small, our joys expand,
Like fractals drawn by fate's own hand.
We swirl in laughter, a vivid spree,
Infinite echoes, just you and me.

A tapestry woven with threads of love,
As stars confide from up above.
Each memory crafted, a colored thread,
In joy we wrap, our hearts are fed.

Heartbeats in Harmony

When silence falls, our hearts align,
In rhythm sweet, your breath is mine.
The pulse of life, a soothing sound,
In tender beats, our souls are found.

A waltz of hearts, in sync we sway,
Through every challenge, come what may.
With every thump, a promise grows,
In harmony, our love glows.

Candlelit Affection

In the flicker of flame, love glows bright,
Whispers of warmth in the soft twilight.
Hands entwined, shadows dance,
A moment of magic, sweet romance.

Each heartbeat a song, softly sung,
In this embrace, we feel forever young.
The world fades away, just us two,
In the candle's light, our love feels new.

Threading Sunlight

Golden rays weave through the trees,
A tapestry of warmth, a gentle breeze.
Leaves whisper secrets, stories untold,
As sunbeams of amber start to unfold.

Nature's embrace, pure and alive,
In this moment, our spirits thrive.
Each step taken, a dance so free,
Threading sunlight, just you and me.

Elysian Glow

Beneath the vast sky, the stars align,
In the hush of night, your hand in mine.
A glow that beckons, soft and bright,
In the realm of dreams, we take flight.

With every heartbeat, the universe sings,
In Elysian fields, we find our wings.
Love eternal, like the moon's soft light,
Together we dance in the depths of night.

Caressed by the Horizon

Where sky meets sea, a painter's delight,
Caressed by the horizon, day turns to night.
Waves whisper tales of distant shores,
In this vastness, my spirit soars.

The sun dips low, colors ablaze,
In this fleeting moment, time gently sways.
With every sunset, a promise we share,
That in love's embrace, we'll always be there.

The Light of Our Souls

In shadows deep, we find our spark,
A gentle glow, igniting the dark.
With every laugh, with every tear,
The light of our souls, forever near.

Through winding paths, love will unfold,
In whispered dreams, our stories told.
Hand in hand, we bravely stride,
With every heartbeat, love's our guide.

Twilight's Loving Brightness

As day departs, the twilight blooms,
A canvas rich with soft perfumes.
The sun's embrace bids night to rise,
In twilight's arms, our spirits fly.

Stars awaken, a dance so sweet,
Where heartbeats harmonize, and dreams meet.
In every hue, in every shade,
Twilight whispers, love won't fade.

Affection Under the Moonscape

Beneath the moon, our shadows play,
In silver light, we find our way.
With every glance, the world feels right,
Affection glows in the peaceful night.

Soft breezes carry whispered vows,
In nature's arms, love surely bows.
The stars above, like diamonds bright,
Guide our hearts under the moon's light.

When Hearts Glow Together

In perfect rhythm, our hearts beat,
Creating warmth, a love so sweet.
Side by side, through life we roam,
In this embrace, we've found our home.

With every sunset, colors blend,
A canvas rich, on love we depend.
When hearts glow bright, shadows depart,
Together we shine, never apart.

Love's Guiding Glow

In twilight's soft embrace, we find our way,
Hearts entwined, like stars in a ballet.
Every whisper, every glance, a spark ignites,
Guided by love through the darkest nights.

Your laughter dances, a melody sweet,
Footsteps synchronized, our souls complete.
In the warmth of your gaze, I lose all fear,
Together we shine, love's light draws near.

Through shadows we wander, hand in hand,
Facing the storms, together we stand.
In the quiet of night, our spirits soar,
A glow everlasting, forevermore.

Embraced by the Cosmos

Beneath the vast heavens, we are but two,
Together we wander, as stardust anew.
Galaxies whisper the secrets of fate,
In the silence of space, our hearts resonate.

With every heartbeat, a constellation forms,
In this cosmic dance, our love transforms.
Celestial bodies align with the flow,
Carried by dreams, love's guiding glow.

Embraced by the cosmos, we lose track of time,
Infinite moments, our spirits climb.
In this grand tapestry, we find our place,
Forever entwined in an endless embrace.

The Light We Share

In the depths of darkness, your smile appears,
A beacon of hope, calming all fears.
Together we journey, side by side,
In every heartbeat, love's light will guide.

With laughter and joy, our spirits ignite,
A flame that burns strong, a radiant light.
Through trials and storms, together we stand,
A luminous bond, perfectly planned.

In moments of silence, your glow shines bright,
A gentle reminder in the still of the night.
The light we share brightens the way,
Carving our path in the light of the day.

Serendipity's Warm Embrace

In the dance of the universe, fate takes her chance,
Two souls colliding in a beautiful dance.
With every glance shared, destiny sings,
Wrapped in serendipity's warm embrace, it brings.

We wandered alone, then found one another,
Like lost little stars, drawn to each other.
In laughter and joy, our spirits align,
Moments like these, truly divine.

Hand in hand, we chase the unknown,
In the light of the moon, our love has grown.
With every heartbeat, serendipity's art,
A journey together, forever to start.

Illuminated Moments

In shadows soft, a whisper sighs,
A spark ignites 'neath twilight skies.
Life's fleeting glance, both bright and brief,
Collecting joy, we weave belief.

Each heartbeat glows like candle's flame,
In quietude, we find our name.
Moments cherished, gently held,
In radiant dreams, our hearts compelled.

Love's Gentle Luminescence

In tender night, love's glow emerges,
A dance of light, where warmth converges.
Softly we lean, our spirits blend,
In cherished whispers, time suspend.

With every touch, the world ignites,
Hearts painted bright in moonlit nights.
In silence shared, a bond we trace,
Love's gentle light, our sacred space.

Flicker of Affection

A flicker sways in dusky air,
An ember breathes, two souls laid bare.
With glances shared, a spark does fly,
In fleeting moments, hearts comply.

Like fireflies dance in twilight hue,
Our laughter rings, a bond so true.
With every glance and every word,
In shadows soft, love's truth is stirred.

Embrace of the Cosmos

Stars alight in endless space,
Galaxies spin, a cosmic grace.
In moonlit arms, the universe sighs,
As dreams take flight, beneath vast skies.

In whispered breaths, we find our way,
Together lost, we choose to stay.
In constellations, we leave our mark,
An embrace eternal, igniting the dark.

Unity in Light

In the dawn where shadows fade,
Hands entwined, a promise made.
Hearts ablaze with shared delight,
Together we embrace the light.

Every path we chose to tread,
Whispers soft, the words unsaid.
In our hearts a chorus sings,
Unity in love, the joy it brings.

Kindred souls in life's embrace,
Finding strength in every space.
Through the storms we bravely fight,
Guided by the stars so bright.

Moments pass like fleeting dreams,
Yet our bond forever gleams.
In each heartbeat, trust ignites,
Together we soar to new heights.

As the sun begins to set,
In our hearts, no room for fret.
Side by side, forever intertwined,
In unity, true peace we find.

Moments That Sparkle

Twinkling stars in evening skies,
Golden laughter, joyful cries.
Every moment, bright and clear,
Memories held so very dear.

Dancing waves by the shoreline,
Captured seconds so divine.
In a glance, a world becomes,
Life's sweet song, our hearts' drums.

Sunlit mornings, gentle streams,
Fleeting time is woven dreams.
As the daylight starts to fade,
Each small spark, a serenade.

Through the silence, whispers play,
Echoes of a perfect day.
In those glimmers, life takes flight,
Moments shine, our hearts alight.

So let us treasure every spark,
In the light, we're never dark.
For in each heartbeat, love will glow,
In moments that forever flow.

The Kiss of Daylight

Morning breaks with softest hues,
Awakens life and dreams anew.
In each ray, a promise sings,
The kiss of daylight gently brings.

Whispers of a brand new start,
Hope ignites within the heart.
Every touch a warm embrace,
As the dawn begins to grace.

Softly melting night's retreat,
Nature dances, life's heartbeat.
With each moment, fresh and bright,
We are touched by golden light.

Through the clouds, the sun will rise,
Painting joy across the skies.
In that glow, our souls unite,
With the kiss of pure daylight.

So let us bask in morning's glow,
And let love's warmth forever flow.
In the sun's embrace, we'll stay,
And cherish each new day.

Embracing the Afterglow

As the sun begins to sink,
In the quiet, we will think.
Moments shared, a sweet reprise,
Embracing joy beneath the skies.

Stars awaken, night's caress,
In the stillness, we confess.
Every memory softly glows,
In the twilight, love bestows.

Hand in hand, we stroll the shore,
Hearts unguarded, seeking more.
In the calm, our dreams will flow,
Together in this afterglow.

Laughter echoes through the night,
In your eyes, the world feels right.
With the moon, our spirits rise,
In the silence, no goodbyes.

So here's to paths we've come to roam,
In each heartbeat, we find home.
In the glow of love, we know,
Together, forever, we'll grow.

Embracing the Twinkle of Tomorrow

In shadows and whispers, we dream,
Hopes rising like stars in the night,
Embracing the moments that gleam,
Our hearts soar with luminous light.

Tomorrow awaits with a smile,
A promise wrapped in dawn's embrace,
We're journeying each precious mile,
Together, we find our true place.

The path ahead sparkles with flair,
Hand in hand, we wander with grace,
In each heartbeat, we feel the air,
Of dreams woven bright in space.

With laughter, we paint the skies blue,
A tapestry made of our wishes,
In the morning, we find what's true,
In each other's eyes, love blooms, kisses.

Embracing the twinkle in sight,
We'll dance through the days yet to come,
With every dawn, we shine so bright,
Finding joy in the beat of the drum.

A Canvas of Light and Love

Upon the canvas, colors swirl,
Dancing under the sun's soft rays,
Each stroke a dream as ribbons twirl,
Creating a masterpiece that stays.

With laughter, we splash vibrant hues,
In a gallery filled with our song,
Every heartbeat a brush, love imbues,
In the silence, where souls belong.

Moments colliding, joy takes flight,
A dance of shadows and bright beams,
Here we find our hearts in the light,
In a world painted from our dreams.

On this canvas, shadows blend too,
We craft our tale in gentle strokes,
Every tear and smile, pure and true,
A story that whispers and invokes.

Together we rise, a sight divine,
With love's brush, we craft every frame,
Each memory strong, like the vine,
In this symphony, forever the same.

Celestial Threads of Affection

In the night sky, threads of light,
Woven with whispers of the stars,
They guide our hearts through the dim night,
Each shimmer tells tales from afar.

Celestial bonds of warmth and grace,
We float on dreams like clouds above,
In every heartbeat, a sacred space,
Filling our souls with threads of love.

Through galaxies, our spirits soar,
Connected by a cosmic embrace,
In this vast universe we explore,
Finding each other in timeless space.

The moon glows softly, our guide near,
As we dance through the cosmic waves,
With every shimmer, we shed our fear,
In the light of the love that saves.

Together, we weave a radiant lace,
Of hopes and dreams, forever spun,
In the tapestry of time and space,
Our hearts beat as one, never done.

The Joy of Shimmering Bonds

In laughter, we find our sweet song,
Shimmering bonds that tie us near,
In moments where hearts belong,
Echoing joy, banishing fear.

With every shared glance, a spark,
Like fireflies dancing in the night,
Illuminating paths from the dark,
Together, we shine in pure light.

Our stories entwined like a vine,
Each twist an adventure we share,
In the warmth of love, we align,
Creating a world that's beyond compare.

Through trials, our laughter resounds,
A melody carried on the breeze,
In the rhythm of life, joy abounds,
In our hearts, we find sweet peace.

With every heartbeat, we celebrate,
The shimmering bonds we hold dear,
In love's embrace, we elevate,
Finding joy in each moment here.

Twilight's Gentle Hold

The sun dips low in the sky,
Casting hues of orange glow.
Whispers dance in evening light,
As shadows start to flow.

Stars awaken in the dusk,
While the moon begins to rise.
Nature hums a soft refrain,
A lullaby for tired eyes.

Birds return to their warm nests,
With gentle coos marking time.
The world finds peace in stillness,
Wrapped in twilight's soft rhyme.

Branches sway with tender grace,
Underneath the velvet skies.
Moments linger, sweet and brief,
As day and night harmonize.

In this dance of light and dark,
Life pauses to take a breath.
A serene embrace of calm,
As we ponder joy and death.

Illuminated Together

Two hearts beating in the night,
Like stars that share their glow.
In every glance, a spark ignites,
Binding us in love's flow.

Laughter echoes through the air,
Each moment pure, divine.
With hands entwined, we journey on,
Leaving the past behind.

The world outside may dim and fade,
But we become the light.
In this cozy, safe embrace,
The darkness turns to bright.

Every whisper, soft and clear,
Paints our dreams across the night.
Together, we forge a path,
Illuminated, hearts in flight.

Through every storm, we stand as one,
With faith that never wanes.
In this union, we find strength,
A love that still remains.

Embrace of the Sunbeams

Morning breaks with golden rays,
Kissing dew upon the grass.
Nature wakes from slumber deep,
As shadows slowly pass.

Sunlight warms the chilled earth,
Inviting life to bloom anew.
Each petal dancing in the breeze,
As colors burst in view.

With arms spread wide, we greet the day,
Grateful for each shining beam.
In this moment, we are free,
Chasing every vibrant dream.

Time unwinds in nature's glow,
While whispers fill the air.
Every heartbeat sings the tune,
Of love beyond compare.

As evening draws with gentle grace,
We revel in the warmth we hold.
Embraced by sunbeams' sweet caress,
Our memories turn to gold.

Cosmic Affinity

In the vastness of the night,
Galaxies spin with grace.
We're but sparks in endless space,
Yet shine in our own place.

Stars collide and drift apart,
Forming bonds across the skies.
In this cosmic symphony,
We find love that never lies.

Nebulas paint a watercolor,
As planets dance in time.
In this universe so grand,
Every heartbeat is a rhyme.

Life flows like a comet's trail,
Bright moments fleeting fast.
Through the void, we make our mark,
A connection meant to last.

As the cosmos breathe and swirl,
We too are caught in flight.
In our souls, a tale unfolds,
Of love and shared starlight.

Harmony of Glowing Hearts

In twilight's grace, we find our song,
Threads of light where we belong.
A dance of spirit, warm and bright,
Together we weave the starlit night.

With every beat, our souls align,
In the silence, love's whispers twine.
The world may fade, but we are here,
In harmony, we conquer fear.

Through gentle storms, we hold our ground,
In sacred moments, beauty's found.
The echoes of our laughter soar,
In glowing hearts, we are much more.

As petals fall, and seasons change,
In tender touch, we rearrange.
Each glance a world, a timeless start,
Forever bound, two glowing hearts.

With every dawn, a promise made,
In shimmering light, our love displayed.
Together we'll face the vast unknown,
In our embrace, we have grown.

Aether's Hug

In the cradle of the sky so wide,
We feel a warmth that won't subside.
Aether's embrace, so soft and true,
Whispering secrets, old and new.

Floating through dreams, we dance in light,
Carried softly by the night.
With every breath, the stars align,
A cosmic bond, forever divine.

Billowing clouds like cotton candy,
A gentle touch, sweet and dandy.
The universe hums our favorite tune,
Wrapped in bliss, beneath the moon.

As stardust swirls, we find our place,
In the infinity of time and space.
Aether's hug, a soft cocoon,
Where heartbeats echo a timeless rune.

With every pulse, our spirits rise,
Connected deeply, we touch the skies.
In this embrace, no shadows fall,
Aether's hug, we feel it all.

Sun-Kissed Whispers

In golden rays, the morning glows,
A symphony of light that flows.
Every beam, a gentle kiss,
Filling our hearts with blissful bliss.

The dawn awakens soft and sweet,
In sunlit dreams, our worlds meet.
With whispered tales from skies above,
We dance in warmth, wrapped in love.

Petals open to the sun's embrace,
Each moment treasured, time won't erase.
With laughter shared, our spirits sing,
In this bright light, we feel the spring.

As twilight falls, the colors blend,
A canvas where the daylight ends.
In dusky hues, our spirits soar,
Sun-kissed whispers, forevermore.

Together we chase the fading day,
In glowing hues, we'll find our way.
With every sunset, we'll renew,
In sun-kissed whispers, just me and you.

Embracing the Glow of Love

In twilight's glow, our hearts entwine,
With gentle whispers, yours and mine.
A sacred space where shadows fade,
In love's embrace, no debts to trade.

With every glance, the warmth ignites,
Flickering flames on cozy nights.
Through every storm, we've found our path,
In laughter's echo, we feel the wrath.

As seasons shift, our love remains,
In vibrant hues, through joys and pains.
With hands held tight, we face the night,
Embracing all, in love's pure light.

In quiet moments, time stands still,
Two souls in harmony, a shared will.
With every heartbeat, futures align,
In the glow of love, you are mine.

Together we bloom, like flowers bright,
In every sunset, you're my light.
Through laughter, tears, and dreams we weave,
Embracing love, we truly believe.

Enveloped in Sunshine

Golden rays dance on my skin,
Whispers of warmth pull me in.
Laughter echoes, joy surrounds,
In this moment, peace abounds.

Fields of daisies, soft and bright,
All my worries take to flight.
Nature's glow, a sweet embrace,
In the sunlight, I find my place.

Time stands still, a cherished gift,
With every ray, my spirits lift.
Subtle breeze, a gentle sigh,
Beneath the vast and endless sky.

Memories woven in light's thread,
In sunshine's glory, fears are shed.
A tranquil heart, with each new dawn,
Together, we rise, forever drawn.

In this warmth, we truly thrive,
Together, in this moment, alive.
A tapestry of golden hue,
Enveloped in sunshine, me and you.

The Light We Share

Stars above in velvet black,
Whispers of love, no turning back.
In your eyes, a glimmer bright,
Together we chase the soft moonlight.

Hands entwined, we walk as one,
Illuminated by the setting sun.
In this silence, our hearts align,
The light we share, forever mine.

Every laugh, every gentle touch,
In this bond, we have so much.
The glow of dreams, a guiding star,
We'll chase the night, no matter how far.

The constellations sing our song,
In this journey, where we belong.
Your warmth, a fire in the cold,
In my heart, your light I hold.

Through the shadows, we dare to blaze,
Together shining through life's maze.
In every heartbeat, love declares,
In every moment, the light we share.

A Blissful Glow

Morning breaks with gentle grace,
Sunlight spills in, warms the space.
Every corner, radiant beam,
Awakening the sweetest dream.

Petals blush in soft display,
Nature's art in bright array.
In this beauty, time stands still,
Wrapped in peace, we're free of will.

Laughter floats on fragrant air,
Every smile, a blissful flare.
In this glow, our spirits dance,
Lost in wonder, caught in chance.

Endless skies, a canvas wide,
With you here, there's naught to hide.
In this moment, all is known,
Together, a blissful glow we've grown.

As twilight draws, the stars appear,
In the night, I hold you near.
In this circle, a love that flows,
Forever in this blissful glow.

Tenderness of the Stars

In the night, so deep and clear,
Whispers of the cosmos near.
With every twinkle, secrets shared,
In the dark, our hearts ensnared.

Cradled in the velvet sky,
Each star a wish, a hopeful sigh.
With you by me, I'm not alone,
In this vastness, we've brightly shone.

Embraced by night, we softly speak,
In every glance, our spirits peak.
Tenderness unfolds like the dawn,
Beneath the sky, where dreams are drawn.

Celestial dances, whispered truths,
In the stillness, the youth of youth.
Together we forge a timeless bond,
In the tenderness of stars, we're fond.

As the night fades into day,
Our love remains, come what may.
In this universe, wide and far,
We find our peace in the stars.

Light's Tender Caress

In the dawn's soft glow, it breaks,
A whisper of warmth as the world wakes.
Golden beams dance through the trees,
Cradling the earth with gentle ease.

Every shadow fades with grace,
As sunlight wraps in its embrace.
Illuminating paths once dark,
Awakening hope, igniting spark.

The flowers bloom, their colors bright,
Touched by love, kissed by light.
A mosaic of nature on display,
In light's tender arms, we find our way.

Through each moment, every glance,
Life's beauty weaves a quiet chance.
To cherish the glow, so divine,
In light's tender caress, we intertwine.

Let it linger, this sacred hour,
Where every heart can feel its power.
With every pulse, we draw anew,
In light's embrace, my soul with you.

With Open Arms to the Sky

Underneath the vast expanse,
I lift my heart, I take a chance.
With open arms, I greet the day,
Inviting dreams to come and stay.

The clouds drift by, a soft parade,
As sunlight pours, the fears allayed.
Each moment fresh as morning dew,
A canvas clear, the sky so blue.

I feel the air, it lifts my soul,
In this embrace, I feel whole.
With arms outstretched, I breathe in deep,
As nature stirs, my spirit leaps.

The horizon calls, a whispered song,
In this great dance, I belong.
With open arms, I reach so high,
Embracing all, with open sky.

So let it rain or let it shine,
In every storm, your hand in mine.
With open hearts, together we fly,
Through life's adventure, you and I.

The Warmth Between Us

On chilly nights, your presence near,
Wraps around me, calms my fear.
With every laugh, warmth does grow,
In tender moments, love's gentle flow.

We share our dreams beneath the stars,
Each whispered hope, no more than ours.
With hands entwined, our spirits blend,
In the warmth between us, time will bend.

Through every storm, through every fight,
Your light shines strong, my guiding light.
Each heartbeat echoes a soft tune,
Beneath the glow of a silver moon.

In quiet spaces, we both find peace,
As love's embrace will never cease.
Through midnight whispers, our souls align,
In the warmth between us, hearts entwine.

Together, side by side we stand,
Facing the world, both hand in hand.
With every smile, every kiss,
The warmth between us, eternal bliss.

Celestial Embraces

In the night's vast, starry dome,
I feel the cosmos, I feel at home.
Celestial whispers, soft and bright,
Embracing dreams in the quiet night.

Galaxies swirl, a cosmic dance,
Each starlit twinkle, a fleeting chance.
The universe hums a lullaby,
In celestial embraces, we reach high.

Constellations map our fate,
Every moment, love creates.
With hands lifted, we touch the sky,
In this connection, we learn to fly.

As meteors blaze, wishes ignite,
We find our place in the endless night.
With every heartbeat, every breath,
Celestial embraces defy death.

So let us gaze until the dawn,
In awe of beauty, we lean on.
With stars as guides, we rise above,
In celestial embraces, we find love.

When Hearts Converge

Two souls meet under the stars,
A whisper of fate pulls them near.
In the quiet, love gently stirs,
Hope blooms where once there was fear.

With each glance, embers ignite,
Promises dance in the night air.
Hand in hand, they rise in flight,
Together, life's burdens they bear.

Their laughter weaves a sweet song,
Melodies crafted with care.
In this union, they belong,
Creating a future to share.

Through storms and sun, they will stand,
Bound by a love that won't fail.
Together, they'll journey hand in hand,
Finding strength in each other's trail.

When hearts converge in perfect grace,
The world fades, all else a blur.
In this moment, they find their place,
Love's magic, a vibrant spur.

Celestial Harmonies

Stars twinkle in the deep night sky,
A symphony of light unfolds.
The moon whispers soft lullabies,
Encircling dreams like precious gold.

Galaxies spin in endless waltz,
Comets dance with fiery trails.
Each note played without any faults,
In the cosmos, harmony prevails.

Clouds drift by in sweet surrender,
Wrapped in the warmth of cosmic flow.
Time pauses, the night grows tender,
As secrets of the universe glow.

Symphonic echoes through the dark,
Where silence sings in perfect tune.
The sky ignites with every spark,
Drawing hearts closer to the moon.

In celestial depths, we find our muse,
A tapestry woven by fate.
In starlit nights, we cannot lose,
Together, we embrace our fate.

The Essence of Brilliance

In every heart, a light does shine,
A spark of gold in shadow's play.
With passion's fire, their souls align,
Creating brilliance day by day.

Dreams burst forth like blooms in spring,
Colors vibrant, rising high.
Hope ascends on silver wing,
In every challenge, they'll fly.

Moments captured in a glance,
The essence of life's sweet allure.
As stars prepare for their grand dance,
Brilliance blooms in hearts pure.

Through every storm and raging sea,
Resilience flourishes and grows.
In this dance of destiny,
The essence of brilliance glows.

And when the dawn breaks soft and sweet,
With courage woven in their seams,
They find joy in each heartbeat,
Chasing after all their dreams.

Caressing Light

Morning rays kiss the waking earth,
Gently painting the world anew.
Each beam whispers of love's worth,
In every hue, the heart feels true.

Soft shadows fade as day unfolds,
Nature's canvas begins to sing.
In radiant warmth, the spirit molds,
Caressing light, a heavenly spring.

Fingers of light weave through the trees,
Where golden leaves dance in delight.
Each whisper carries on the breeze,
Caressing shadows, taking flight.

As sunsets paint the skies with gold,
A tender embrace from day to night.
In the gloaming, tales are told,
Of love and warmth in caressing light.

In every moment, let us bask,
Find solace in the glow we see.
For in love's embrace, we unmask,
The beauty of eternity.

Enchanted Radiance

In twilight's tender grace,
Stars shimmer like dreams,
Whispers of magic dance,
In the soft moonbeams.

The trees wear silken veils,
As shadows intertwine,
A melody of night,
In harmony divine.

Gentle breezes sigh low,
Through the fragrant blooms,
Awakening the heart,
Dispelling dark glooms.

Each petal holds a tale,
Of love's pure embrace,
In the garden of night,
Time finds its own pace.

With every breath we take,
Enchantment unfolds wide,
In this sacred moment,
Where dreams can't hide.

The Warmth of Togetherness

In the glow of the fire,
Laughter fills the air,
Every heart is lighter,
In this moment we share.

Cups clink in the night,
To memories we've spun,
Every story whispered,
In the warmth of the sun.

Together we find joy,
In the simple things,
From raindrops on windows,
To the songs that life sings.

With hands held so tight,
We bravely face the storm,
In the love that we carry,
We find our true form.

As stars twinkle above,
Guiding us along,
In the warmth of togetherness,
We know we belong.

Chasing the Horizon

With each step I take,
Footprints in the sand,
The horizon calls softly,
With dreams in hand.

Streaks of gold and blue,
Paint the vast expanse,
A dance of light and shadow,
Invites me to chance.

Whispers of the sea,
Guide me on my way,
Every wave that crashes,
Sings of a new day.

Mountains loom ahead,
Majestic and grand,
I chase the horizon,
With hope as my brand.

For beyond the skyline,
Lies a world unknown,
With courage as my compass,
I'll wander alone.

Serene Glow

In the quiet of dawn,
Light begins to rise,
Kissing the world gently,
With soft lullabies.

Fields wrapped in stillness,
Dewdrops gleam like jewels,
Nature's calm embrace,
In its language of rules.

The sun paints the sky,
With hues of peach and rose,
Each moment a treasure,
That the heart well knows.

Birds sing the dawn chorus,
In notes pure and true,
Awakening the world,
In a vibrant hue.

As the day unfolds,
In serene glow we find,
Peace in every heartbeat,
Together, intertwined

A Symphony of Lightheartedness

In bright fields where laughter grows,
The sun shines down, the wildwind blows.
Dancing shadows, vibrant hues,
With every step, we sing our blues.

Joy spills forth like rivers wide,
With every heartbeat, dreams collide.
Whispers of play, a carefree sigh,
Under the canvas of an endless sky.

Children's laughter, a sweet refrain,
Echoes through the golden grain.
In this moment, all feels bright,
A symphony of pure delight.

Clouds drift like thoughts, soft and light,
Each glance exchanged, a spark ignites.
In this realm, where spirits soar,
We revel in what we adore.

Together we weave, a vibrant thread,
A tapestry where worries shed.
Hand in hand, we chase the day,
In a dance of life, we freely sway.

Glowing Whispers

Stars twinkle softly in the night,
Whispers of secrets take flight.
Each glow a promise, a wish cast,
In the stillness, we hold fast.

Moonbeams kiss the silent ground,
In the quiet, joy is found.
Dreams unfold like petals rare,
Glowing whispers fill the air.

As shadows play their graceful game,
Eager hearts, we feel the same.
In the darkness, we find light,
Wrapped in warmth, we feel so right.

Glimmers of hope in every sigh,
With every glance, we touch the sky.
Together we bask in night's embrace,
Glowing softly in this sacred space.

Within the still, our thoughts entwine,
In glowing whispers, hearts align.
Together we dream, together we soar,
In harmony, we can't ask for more.

Warmth of Light

Sunrise spills through open blinds,
A golden glow that gently finds.
It drapes the world in hues so bright,
Caressing hearts with pure delight.

Morning's breath, so fresh and clear,
With every ray, it draws us near.
Embraced by warmth, we start anew,
In the light, we feel the true.

Gentle warmth upon our skin,
A tender promise deep within.
The day awakens, life does start,
With every ray, it fills the heart.

As shadows fade and colors blend,
In this warmth, we find a friend.
Together basking in the glow,
In the warmth, our spirits grow.

In every corner, joy ignites,
Life dances in the morning lights.
With open arms, we greet the day,
In warmth of light, we laugh and play.

Embrace of Dawn

Blue hues brush against the sky,
As dawn awakens, we sigh.
With gentle hands, it parts the night,
Embracing worlds in soft twilight.

Birdsong rises, pure and sweet,
Nature stirs to the rhythm, neat.
A tender blush spreads, like a song,
In dawn's embrace, where we belong.

Golden rays peek through the trees,
Stirring dreams in warm, soft breeze.
This sacred hour, a gift to share,
A moment held in tender care.

Hope ignites with each new day,
In the dawn, worries fade away.
With hearts wide open, we find our place,
In the embrace of dawn's soft grace.

Together we dance in morning's light,
Chasing shadows, holding tight.
In every heartbeat, love's refrain,
We rise renewed, without a chain.

Gilded Hugs

In the dusk's warm embrace, light glows,
Whispers of love in soft, tender prose.
Hearts intertwine, a sacred dance,
In gilded hues, they find their chance.

Time melts away in the twilight's grace,
Every moment cherished, a sweet embrace.
Underneath the stars, dreams take flight,
In golden moments, everything feels right.

The world fades softly, just us two,
Wrapped in warmth where love feels new.
Gilded hugs in a soft sunset,
In this perfect moment, we won't forget.

Hands softly placed, fingers entwined,
In unity found, our hearts aligned.
Together we dwell in this sacred space,
Gilded hugs, our love's embrace.

With every heartbeat, our spirits soar,
In this timeless hush, we crave more.
Whispers of magic linger like a song,
In gilded hugs, we both belong.

Dance of the Fireflies

In the twilight glow, they begin to ignite,
Tiny lanterns twinkling in the night.
Graceful movements, a waltz through the air,
In the soft summer breeze, love's light lies bare.

Each flicker a promise, a soft, sweet chance,
In shadows and whispers, they twirl and dance.
Nature's own ballet, a symphony bright,
Under the canopy of the velvet night.

Hearts beat in rhythm with the glow all around,
Lost in this moment, euphoria found.
A tapestry woven of glow and delight,
In the dance of the fireflies, love feels right.

Eternal the magic, in luminescent skies,
With every soft flicker, a sweet surprise.
Together we twirl, our souls intertwined,
In this dance of the fireflies, love is defined.

As night drifts away and dawn gently blooms,
We'll carry this light when the daylight looms.
In the heart's quiet whispers, we'll always know,
The dance of the fireflies, a sparkling glow.

Resplendent Affection

The sun paints the sky in hues of gold,
Love's gentle warmth, a story unfolds.
In resplendent moments, we find our way,
In each treasured glance, in the light of day.

Soft rustling leaves in the whispering breeze,
With every heartbeat, our souls find ease.
In the glow of affection, our spirits soar high,
Underneath the vast, endless sky.

Two souls entwined in this timeless dance,
Every soft touch, a sweet romance.
With laughter and joy in every reflection,
We cradle the beauty of resplendent affection.

Through storms and trials, hand in hand we tread,
In the garden of dreams where love is spread.
In the bloom of the heart, a vibrant collection,
Forever bound by resplendent affection.

Time may change, but our love will stay bright,
In the canvas of life, our colors ignite.
With joy in our hearts and a deep connection,
We cherish the warmth of resplendent affection.

Golden Threads

Woven through time, our lives intertwine,
With every shared moment, a sweet design.
In laughter and love, the tapestry grows,
With golden threads that time gently sows.

Each stitch a memory, a love that we hold,
In the fabric of life, our stories unfold.
Through trials and triumphs, our colors inspire,
As golden threads weave a tapestry, higher.

In shadows and sunlight, through joy and strife,
We sew together the quilt of our life.
Every thread a promise, bright and bold,
In the warmth of our journey, a love to be told.

With every day passing, the pattern grows clear,
In the quilt of our dreams, we hold each other near.
Together we stitch the dreams we have fed,
In the heart of our home, golden threads are spread.

And when the days fade, and the nights draw near,
In the warmth of our love, there's nothing to fear.
A tapestry woven, in love's perfect shed,
Forever we flourish with golden threads.

The Light That Binds

In shadows cast, we find our way,
A flicker bright, it bends the gray.
Through troubled nights, hope starts to shine,
Together still, your hand in mine.

A spark ignites, our hearts entwined,
With every step, our souls aligned.
In whispered tones, our dreams take flight,
In love's embrace, we chase the light.

Serenity in Starlight

Under the vast, unyielding skies,
Whispers of peace begin to rise.
In gentle night, our fears dissolve,
In starlit dreams, we find resolve.

Each twinkling spark ignites a song,
A lullaby where we belong.
In silent grace, we holding tight,
Awake our souls in soft twilight.

Woven in Warmth

In moments shared, hearts weave the thread,
A tapestry, where love is spread.
Through every laugh, through every tear,
We build a bond that draws us near.

In cozy corners, warmth ignites,
With whispered hopes on chilly nights.
Together, we light the winter's end,
In each embrace, our spirits mend.

Glimmering Moments of Togetherness

Within the crowd, your eyes I meet,
A fleeting glance, our hearts repeat.
In every laugh, in every glance,
We find a spark, we take a chance.

The world fades out, it's just us two,
In twilight's glow, the sky so blue.
Each moment shared, a treasure rare,
In glimmering light, we breathe the air.

Embrace of the Warm Breeze

The gentle whispers of the air,
Carry secrets everywhere.
A soothing touch upon the skin,
Where love and nature both begin.

Soft petals sway, they intertwine,
With every breath, our hearts align.
The world around us fades to gray,
As warmth of love lights up the way.

In each caress, the sun will rise,
With every laugh, our spirits rise.
The warm breeze hums a sweet refrain,
In its embrace, we drift like grain.

A fragrant path beneath our feet,
Every heartbeat, a melody sweet.
Through fields of gold, we wander free,
In nature's charm, you're here with me.

Together lost, two souls as one,
In the warm breeze, we come undone.
The universe within our grasp,
In this moment, we hold and clasp.

A Dance Beneath the Stars

The night unfolds, a velvet dream,
With twinkling lights, a silver beam.
We twirl and spin 'neath cosmic glow,
The rhythm of the night winds slow.

With every step, a charm unfolds,
In whispered tales and secrets told.
The moon above, a guiding lamp,
Our hearts ablaze, our spirits damp.

Each star a witness to our glee,
As constellations dance with me.
In the cool breeze, our laughter sings,
A tapestry of joy it brings.

Our shadows sway on endless ground,
A silent bond forever bound.
With hands entwined, we find our place,
In this waltz, we leave no trace.

So here we glide, no fear, no doubt,
In celestial light we twist about.
A dance of wonder, hearts set free,
In the night's embrace, just you and me.

The Dawn's Loving Touch

A soft awakening in the sky,
With hues of pink that softly lie.
The dawn creeps in with tender grace,
A gentle kiss on every face.

The world ignites with golden glow,
Whispers of warmth in morning's flow.
Birds share songs to greet the day,
As night's shadows slowly sway.

With each new beam, our dreams renew,
An invitation for love to brew.
The heart beats loud, the spirit sways,
In morning light, we find our ways.

A soft embrace, a loving glance,
Embarking on this new day's dance.
Joy paints the canvas of our path,
In dawn's sweet glow, we feel the warmth.

So let us cherish every ray,
And share our love in light's ballet.
Together waiting for what's to touch,
The promise of a day that's much.

Illuminated Affection

In every spark, a glimmer shines,
The magic of our hearts entwined.
With every glance, a story told,
In illuminated nights so bold.

We dance in shadows, hand in hand,
With whispered dreams that softly strand.
The twinkling stars, our only guide,
In this realm where love won't hide.

Through moments shared, both near and far,
You are my light, my brightest star.
As lanterns glow with amber hue,
In stillness, love feels ever true.

A warmth that lingers in the air,
An endless bond beyond compare.
With every heartbeat, our spirits sing,
In the glow of what our hearts will bring.

Together wrapped in silver beams,
We'll chase the night and all our dreams.
Through illuminated paths we stroll,
In love's embrace, we find our soul.

Soulful Illumination

In the quiet night, the stars align,
A whisper of hope, like vintage wine.
Hearts open wide to the softest breeze,
Illuminated souls find their peace.

Through shadows of doubt, we wander still,
With dreams aglow, hearts gently fill.
The moon's warm glow reflects our grace,
A journey of love, in this sacred space.

As dawn approaches, colors blend,
Every note we shared, every hand we lend.
In every heartbeat, a spark ignites,
Together we rise, in boundless heights.

The melody flows, in symphonic time,
Words dance like fire, in rhythm and rhyme.
With every touch, we break the night,
Soulful illumination, our guiding light.

And when twilight fades, we'll stand as one,
In the embrace of love, our battles won.
Eternal connection, like rivers run,
In the tapestry of life, we are spun.

Embracing the Golden Hour

As the sun dips low, the world aglow,
Fingers entwined, with love we sow.
Golden rays wrap 'round our hearts,
A fleeting moment, where beauty starts.

Shadows grow long, yet warmth ignites,
In every gaze, a thousand lights.
Laughter echoes through the air,
Time stands still, in this love we share.

Nature's canvas, painted so bright,
Brushstrokes of gold, a pure delight.
We steal a kiss while the sky ablaze,
Embracing this hour in a blissful haze.

The horizon whispers secrets untold,
In every breath, stories unfold.
In this golden glow, we find our way,
With every sunset, our hearts will stay.

Bound by dreams, we'll chase the sun,
In this radiant glow, we become one.
Forever intertwined till the night does call,
In the golden hour, we'll embrace it all.

Hues of Happiness

In the garden where colors bloom,
Bright petals dance, dispelling gloom.
Here joy spills forth, like morning dew,
Hues of happiness, ever true.

Golden yellows, shades of cheer,
Whispers of laughter, so crystal clear.
Every flower a tale, a song, a sigh,
In this vibrant world, we learn to fly.

Pastel dreams in a sky so blue,
Every moment shared, a memory new.
Sunshine kisses on gentle leaves,
Hues of happiness, the heart believes.

In the dappled light, we spin and twirl,
With every smile, our sorrows unfurl.
The palette of life, in shades divine,
Together we shine, forever entwined.

Let's chase rainbows, with arms wide apart,
In this colorful world, we find our heart.
In every brushstroke, let's paint our way,
Hues of happiness, come what may.

A Symphony of Light and Love

In the twilight glow, whispers arise,
A symphony plays beneath the skies.
Notes of affection fill the air,
Melodies of love, beyond compare.

Each heartbeat pulses with vibrant sound,
In this harmony, we are unbound.
With every chord, the universe sings,
A tapestry woven of divine things.

Under starlit skies, our spirits dance,
Lost in the rhythm of a timeless trance.
Guiding us softly, like evening's sigh,
A symphony of light, as days go by.

With every crescendo, dreams take flight,
We craft our story under the night.
In the stillness, love's essence thrives,
A symphony of souls, forever alive.

As dawn beckons with its golden hue,
The music lingers in all we do.
Together we wander, hand in glove,
In this life's symphony, light and love.

Woven Warmth

In the hush of night, hearts combine,
Threads of laughter, gently twine.
Whispers soft like a tender breeze,
Wrapped in love, we find our ease.

Fireside dreams, they flicker bright,
Shared stories dance in the fading light.
Every glance a silent song,
In your arms, I feel I belong.

Through the storms, our fabric holds,
In vibrant hues, our tale unfolds.
Woven tightly, we stand as one,
Forever joined, 'neath moon and sun.

Seasons change but we remain,
A tapestry free of pain.
Each thread a vow, a promise made,
In every warmth, our love displayed.

So let us wrap in this embrace,
Finding home in each other's space.
Woven warmth, a comfort grand,
Together in this timeless land.

Dawn's Tender Glow

Morning breaks with a gentle sigh,
Colors swirl in the waking sky.
Softly kissed by golden rays,
The world awakens, begins to blaze.

Birds take flight on wings of song,
Nature hums a tune so strong.
Whispers of light dance on leaves,
As day unfolds, the heart believes.

In the hush, new dreams arise,
Glistening dew with sparkling eyes.
Each moment fresh, a brand new start,
Dawn's embrace, it fills the heart.

Together we greet this tender scene,
Hands entwined, two souls serene.
With every step, we chase the sun,
In dawn's glow, we are but one.

The world awakens from its night,
In every corner, warmth and light.
Dawn's tender glow, a blissful show,
Together in its soft, warm flow.

Luminescence of Togetherness

Beneath the stars, two hearts ignite,
A luminous bond, glowing bright.
In each laughter, a spark is found,
Together we rise from the ground.

Flickering moments, love's embrace,
In every shadow, we find our place.
The night sings with a joyful tune,
Wrapped in the glow of a silver moon.

Fires burn low, but embers stay,
In the warmth of love, we choose to play.
Colors merge in a vibrant dance,
In every glance, a dream, a chance.

Through trials faced, we stand as one,
Luminescence bright like the morning sun.
Every heartbeat, a cherished sound,
In this togetherness, we are found.

In the hush of night, our souls combine,
A radiant path, forever mine.
Luminescent love, we freely share,
Together awash in the evening air.

Celestial Bonding

Under the vast and starry sky,
Whispers of the universe draw nigh.
In cosmic dance, two souls align,
A bond transcending space and time.

Galaxies spin, yet we remain,
In the infinite, we break the chain.
Stardust trails mark our embrace,
With every heartbeat, we find our place.

Constellations tell our tale,
In twilight's glow, we will not pale.
Celestial rhythms guide our way,
A love eternal, come what may.

Through the night, our spirits soar,
In this bonding, we want for nothing more.
Infinity calls, but still we glow,
In the depths of love's warm flow.

So take my hand beneath the stars,
Together we'll weave the moon and Mars.
Celestial bonding, a cosmic fate,
In this vast world, we resonate.

The Touch of Warmth

In the chill of twilight air,
Soft whispers linger everywhere.
A gentle breeze begins to kiss,
Hearts awaken, feeling bliss.

Fingers brush like autumn leaves,
In their dance, the spirit weaves.
Colors blend in sunset's glow,
A warmth ignites, begins to flow.

Cocooned in dreams, we sway and weave,
In this moment, we believe.
All sorrows fade, the shadows thin,
Together here, our souls begin.

Each heartbeat thrums a secret tune,
In silken threads, the stars attune.
Boundless skies and open hearts,
From the warmth, new life imparts.

Tomorrow brings a fresh embrace,
With yearning smiles, our fears erase.
Under the sun, we'll freely roam,
The touch of warmth, our endless home.

An Embrace of Light and Love

Stars awaken in the night,
Casting down their gentle light.
In this cosmos, we reside,
Together, side by side.

Shadows dance, a fleeting game,
In your eyes, I find my aim.
Every glance, a spark ignites,
Filling darkness with delights.

Hand in hand, we chase the dawn,
Where every pain, we'll cast and pawn.
With laughter wrapped in pure embrace,
The world rewrites its endless space.

In this warmth, we come alive,
With love and grace, we always thrive.
Connected souls in harmony,
An endless song, our tapestry.

Through whispers soft, we find our way,
Guided by the light of day.
In every heartbeat, love will gleam,
In our embrace, we chase the dream.

Ethereal Connection

In silence deep, we softly breathe,
A tapestry of light we weave.
Beyond the realm where shadows lie,
In whispered hopes, our spirits fly.

Each glance shared, a fleeting spark,
In shadowed corners, brightens dark.
When hands touch, the world stands still,
An echo in the heart, a thrill.

Voices blend like songs in night,
Each note a gentle promise bright.
We dance on air, in sacred space,
A unity none can replace.

With every laugh, our spirits soar,
In boundless joy, we seek for more.
A magic thread, a bond so true,
In this connection, me and you.

As time flows on like rivers wide,
In memory's heart, we'll always glide.
An ethereal touch, soft as dove,
In this dance, we find our love.

Glowing Promises

In twilight's glow, our secrets hide,
Promises whispered, never denied.
With each soft word, our spirits wake,
In the silence, a bond we make.

Stars above, like candles bright,
Guide our hearts through endless night.
With every dream, a promise grows,
In the light, our love bestows.

Gentle warmth against my skin,
In your gaze, the world begins.
Future paths extend in view,
In every step, it's me and you.

Through storms and calm, we'll stay the course,
Hand in hand, a steady force.
In glowing embers, our hopes ignite,
Together we chase the morning light.

So here we stand, with open hearts,
Embracing all that life imparts.
With glowing promises, we'll write,
A story of love, forever bright.

Luminous Connections

In twilight's embrace, we find our way,
Threads of gold shine where shadows lay.
Hearts intertwine with laughter and grace,
Brightened spirits in this sacred space.

Whispers linger in the evening glow,
Carried softly where gentle winds flow.
Eyes that sparkle, a dance of delight,
Unveiling the stars on this magical night.

With each gentle touch, our souls align,
Woven together, your heart and mine.
Time stands still as we savor the now,
Luminous bonds that we can't disavow.

We rise like fireflies, unbound and free,
Lighting the world with our harmony.
Together we journey, through dreams we sail,
Braving the storms, we shall never fail.

In this radiant dance, we boldly shine,
Every heartbeat echoes, your hand in mine.
As daybreak approaches, our spirits ignite,
Forever connected in love's pure light.

Caress of Sunbeams

Morning's kiss on dew-kissed leaves,
Nature's symphony as daylight weaves.
Golden rays play in fields so wide,
A caress of warmth in which we confide.

Underneath the arching trees,
Soft whispers drift on a gentle breeze.
Sunbeams dance on our upturned face,
Embracing us in their warm embrace.

With every step, the world comes alive,
In this radiant glow, we thrive.
Time slows down, as shadows retreat,
In this golden hour, our hearts do meet.

Moments are sacred, each one divine,
Seasons change, yet love's light will shine.
A tapestry of laughter and song,
In the arms of the sun, where we belong.

We'll chase the colors of the setting sun,
Hand in hand, we continue to run.
A lifetime of memories, bright and bold,
In every sunbeam, our love unfolds.

Shimmering Hearts

In the quiet night, when dreams take flight,
Shimmering hearts share warmth and light.
A melody played on the strings of fate,
Two souls entwined, it's never too late.

With whispers soft as the midnight air,
Promises bloom like flowers rare.
Each glance exchanged ignites a spark,
Lighting the shadows, kindling the dark.

Together we wander through starlit nights,
Guided by love and celestial sights.
Silent music flows through our veins,
In this dance of joy, we break the chains.

Through every heartbeat, we feel the rush,
A symphony sweet in this tender hush.
With every embrace, the world disappears,
Just the two of us, no worries, no fears.

As dawn approaches, we linger still,
Wrapped in the warmth of our shared will.
Shimmering hearts will forever reside,
In the tapestry woven by love's tide.

Ecstasy of Illumination

When shadows yield to the morning glow,
A dance of light begins to flow.
Awakening dreams with colors divine,
The ecstasy of illumination, truly mine.

Bright horizons stretch beyond the dawn,
Every heartbeat, a vibrant song.
In this moment, time seems to pause,
Caught in the magic of nature's laws.

Together we rise, as spirits align,
Lost in the brilliance of love's design.
With every glance, the universe sings,
Celebrating joy that pure love brings.

The path ahead glimmers with hope,
Guiding us through each curve and slope.
In the face of darkness, our light will beam,
Navigating the world, we chase our dream.

As night falls softly, stars start to gleam,
Whispers of love flow like a stream.
In the ecstasy found in this sacred space,
We find forever in each embrace.

The Glimmer of Us

In twilight's soft embrace, we meet,
A whisper of hope beneath our feet.
Stars align in a delicate dance,
In this fleeting moment, we take the chance.

With every glance, our hearts ignite,
In shadows and dreams, we find the light.
The world may fade, but here we stand,
Together, forever, hand in hand.

Through valleys deep, and mountains high,
We chase the dawn, as time slips by.
With laughter shared and secrets kept,
In the glimmer of us, our promises weeps.

Among the echoes of the night,
Our voices blend, a sweet delight.
Bound by love, we redefine,
The glimmer of us, a love divine.

And as the stars begin to fade,
In every heartbeat, a choice is made.
To nurture dreams, and never rush,
In the gentle glimmer, we find our hush.

Kindred Lights

In the quiet of the evening glow,
Two hearts align, a vibrant show.
With every spark that we ignite,
We weave a story, kindred lights.

Through tangled paths and winding ways,
Together we dance, in sunlit rays.
Each moment shared, a cherished gift,
In laughter's echo, our souls uplift.

The universe sings, a timeless tune,
Under the watchful eye of the moon.
As dreams take flight, we soar above,
In the glow of the night, we find our love.

With every tear and every smile,
The road is long, but worth the while.
Hand in hand, in quiet night,
We are bound as one, kindred lights.

Through storms and trials, we'll stay near,
In every silence, we will hear.
For love's a flame that never fades,
In our hearts' embrace, kindred lights cascade.

Undying Warmth

In the chill of night, your smile glows,
A fire within, as the cold wind blows.
With every touch, my worries cease,
In your presence, I find my peace.

Through memories shared, we weave our past,
A tapestry of love, built to last.
Even as seasons begin to change,
Our hearts entwined, they will not estrange.

In the quiet moments, our spirits rise,
A love so deep, it defies the skies.
With laughter ringing, and stories told,
In your arms, I let go of the cold.

Through life's tempests, our bond remains,
A shelter built from joys and pains.
Every heartbeat writes a part,
Of undying warmth within our hearts.

So let the winds of fortune blow,
For in your heart, I've found my home.
With love eternal, we shall embark,
In every heartbeat, undying spark.

Embraced by Daydreams

In the soft cradle of morning's light,
We dance on the edges of dreams so bright.
With whispers of hope woven in air,
Embraced by love, we dream without care.

As twilight descends, our stories unfold,
With each fluttering moment, our love grows bold.
In daydreams' embrace, we soar on high,
Two souls intertwined beneath the vast sky.

Through gardens of laughter, we wander free,
In every shared glance, a silent decree.
Together we weave what life can't take,
Embraced by daydreams, our hearts awake.

With every heartbeat, a promise we make,
In love's gentle folds, there's no heartache.
From dawn till dusk, we chase the sun,
In dreams embraced, we become as one.

So let us linger in this blissful haze,
In the warmth of affection, our spirits blaze.
For as long as stars in the heavens gleam,
We'll dance forever, embraced by daydreams.

Illuminated Souls

In the quiet of the night,
Dreams take flight, hearts ignite.
Stars whisper secrets of old,
Guiding us towards the bold.

Together we chase the glow,
Through the valleys we shall flow.
With every step, spirits rise,
Illuminated in the skies.

Wonders dance in silver beams,
Awakening our hidden dreams.
In this moment, pure and whole,
We find peace within our soul.

Carry the light, let it shine,
In each heart, a spark divine.
With love's warmth as our guide,
Illuminated, side by side.

Together we weave the night,
In harmony, a future bright.
Every soul, a vibrant hue,
Illuminated, me and you.

Beyond the Shadows

In the dusk, fears come alive,
But within us, dreams survive.
Past the shadows, hope does gleam,
Guiding us through every dream.

Silent battles, fought and lost,
But strength rises, never tossed.
With every breath, we will stand,
Beyond the dark, we take our hand.

Whispers of dawn break the gloom,
Filling hearts with sweet perfume.
Footsteps taken, brave and bold,
Beyond the shadows, stories told.

In the sunlight, we emerge,
With each heartbeat, we converge.
Together, we are not alone,
Beyond the shadows, light is grown.

Fear dissolves like morning dew,
As courage blooms in vibrant blue.
In unity, we find our song,
Beyond the shadows, we belong.

Emblazoned Hearts

Fires burn within us bright,
Every heartbeat, pure delight.
In a world that seeks to part,
We unite with emblazoned hearts.

Colors vibrant, hues that blend,
In each laugh, our spirits mend.
Through the storms, we stand as one,
Emblazoned hearts, brightly spun.

With every step, our passions rise,
In the dance beneath the skies.
A tapestry of love and light,
Emblazoned hearts in purest sight.

When the night seems cold and long,
In our hearts, we sing a song.
Together weaving dreams anew,
Emblazoned hearts, forever true.

Let the flames of love ignite,
In our souls, a guiding light.
With every story that imparts,
We stand strong with emblazoned hearts.

Embrace of the Solstice

Whispers tell of change and light,
In the solstice, day meets night.
Nature dances, cycles renew,
Embrace the moment, pure and true.

Gather 'round, let shadows fade,
In this realm, memories made.
With the sun as our own guide,
In its warmth, we will abide.

Together, we greet the dawn,
In its glow, our fears are gone.
Holding hands, we stand as one,
Embrace of the solstice begun.

Radiant skies, colors blend,
With each heartbeat, we transcend.
In this unity, we rise,
Embrace the solstice, kiss the skies.

Celebrate the turning year,
In the magic, find your cheer.
With each heartbeat, let love flow,
Embrace the solstice, let us grow.

Illumination in Tender Moments

In shadows soft we find our light,
A gentle glow that feels just right.
With every glance, hearts intertwine,
In tender moments, love will shine.

The silence speaks, a sweet refrain,
A dance of whispers, joy and pain.
With every beat, our souls align,
In tender moments, love will shine.

The world outside may rush and chase,
Yet here we find our sacred space.
In fleeting time, we still define,
In tender moments, love will shine.

A fleeting sigh, a knowing glance,
In every touch, we find romance.
With warmth that pulses, pure and fine,
In tender moments, love will shine.

So let us rest where hearts abide,
Beneath the stars, where dreams reside.
In sweet embrace, we redefine,
In tender moments, love will shine.

The Warmth Between Us

The evening sun caresses skin,
A moment shared, where dreams begin.
With laughter bright, and spirits high,
The warmth between us will not die.

In quiet hours, our hearts converse,
Words unspoken, yet they immerse.
Like shadows close, with love to fly,
The warmth between us will not die.

As seasons change, and time moves on,
This bond remains, a steadfast dawn.
No distance long can justify,
The warmth between us will not die.

Through storms and trials, we will stand,
Each sturdy heart, a willing hand.
No storm can break what we rely,
The warmth between us will not die.

So let us weave a life anew,
With threads of love, both brave and true.
Together always, you and I,
The warmth between us will not die.

Shimmering Threads of Affection

Like stars that twinkle in the night,
Your love reflects a radiant light.
In soft embraces, dreams take flight,
Shimmering threads bind day and night.

Each whispered word, a silken strand,
A bond that grows, hand in hand.
Together we weave, so pure, so bright,
Shimmering threads bind day and night.

Through every trial, our love will string,
A melody of hope we sing.
With every heartbeat, soft and slight,
Shimmering threads bind day and night.

In laughter shared and tears that fall,
We find our way through it all.
In every glance, our hearts ignite,
Shimmering threads bind day and night.

So let us cherish this sweet art,
The tapestry stitched, you and I part.
In timeless dance, our spirits light,
Shimmering threads bind day and night.

Celestial Caress

In twilight's glow, we find our space,
As whispers flow in soft embrace.
With every breath, the stars confess,
A love adorned, a celestial caress.

The moonlight dances on your skin,
A symphony of souls within.
In cosmic rhythms, we find our rest,
A love adorned, a celestial caress.

With every heartbeat, time stands still,
Our spirits soar upon the hill.
Together we chase the world's jest,
A love adorned, a celestial caress.

As constellations keep their watch,
We weave our dreams without a botch.
In every moment, we are blessed,
A love adorned, a celestial caress.

So let us reach for what is true,
In endless skies, it's me and you.
With every star, our hearts invest,
A love adorned, a celestial caress.

The Light That Unites

In the dawn's soft embrace,
We gather as one,
Shadows fade, hopes chase,
Heartbeats in tune, begun.

Threads of gold intertwine,
Across the vast divide,
In every smile, we shine,
Together we abide.

Moments shared like a flame,
In whispers, love ignites,
Through laughter, we reclaim,
The warmth on winter nights.

Every tear, every cheer,
Builds the bridge so wide,
With you, I have no fear,
In this journey, we ride.

So let the lanterns glow,
Guiding paths we take,
In the light, we will grow,
Together, hearts awake.

Glimmers of Togetherness

Stars whisper soft and bright,
In the canvas of the night,
Each twinkle tells a tale,
Of love that will prevail.

Hands held tightly in trust,
In this bond, we find strength,
Through the storms, we'll adjust,
Together, we go the length.

Moments of pure delight,
Like fireflies in the dark,
Guiding our way each night,
With a gentle spark.

Even when shadows loom,
And the path seems unclear,
We'll find light in the gloom,
With you, I have no fear.

In the heart of our dreams,
We weave a tapestry,
In the glimmer, it seems,
Love's true artistry.

A Symphony of Light

In the quiet of the morn,
When the world starts to wake,
Together, we are reborn,
In each breath that we take.

Notes of laughter ascend,
Creating our sweet song,
Every heart becomes friend,
In this harmony strong.

Dancing under the sun,
With shadows far away,
Every battle we've won,
In the light of the day.

Together, we compose,
A melody of grace,
With every note, love grows,
In this bright, shared space.

As we close our day's tome,
Under the twilight's hue,
In this light, we find home,
Forever, me and you.

Unfolding in Brilliance

With each dawn's tender kiss,
New beginnings arise,
In the warmth, we find bliss,
Beneath the endless skies.

Petals of hope unfurl,
In gardens of our dreams,
Each moment's a pearl,
As bright as moonlit beams.

In the tapestry we weave,
Every thread speaks of love,
Together, we believe,
In the gifts from above.

Through the storms that may pass,
Our light will never dim,
In the warmth of your glass,
Together, we can swim.

As the night falls again,
With stars shining bright,
In your eyes, I can pen,
The story of our light

Flickering Hearts' Connection

In shadows cast by soft twilight,
Two hearts align, a spark ignites.
With every beat, a story told,
A bond that flourishes, bright and bold.

Through whispers shared in gentle night,
They weave a tapestry of light.
A dance of souls in sweet refrain,
Together weather joy and pain.

Each glance a flame, a fleeting spark,
Illuminating love's deep arc.
In silence held, the world fades away,
Flickering hearts shall ever stay.

In every sigh, a promise made,
In every touch, the fears allayed.
They find their way through stormy seas,
Flickering hearts, forever free.

With every dawn, their spirits rise,
Chasing dreams beneath the skies.
A connection born, a love so pure,
In flickers bright, their hearts endure.

A Glimpse of Starlight

Beneath the veil of midnight's glow,
A glimpse of starlight starts to flow.
Whispers of hope in the cool night air,
Promises linger, sweet and rare.

Each star a wish, a dream set free,
Guiding hearts to what will be.
In the quiet, magic unfolds,
A universe woven in silken gold.

With every twinkle, secrets shared,
The cosmos sings, all souls ensnared.
In this moment, time stands still,
A glimpse of starlight, hearts to fill.

With every shadow, a light emerges,
An echo of love's gentle urges.
Together they find a guiding light,
In the darkness, stars feel bright.

As dawn approaches, the stars fade slow,
Yet in their hearts, the embers glow.
A glimpse of starlight, forever drawn,
Guiding dreamers till the dawn.

Cherished Radiance

In every smile, a spark appears,
A cherished radiance, beyond the years.
It glows in laughter, warms the soul,
Binding hearts to make them whole.

Sun-kissed moments, dancing light,
Through every shadow, pure delight.
A treasure found in whispered dreams,
Shining bright in moonlit beams.

With every heartbeat, love takes flight,
Cherished radiance, a guiding light.
In gentle holds and tender sighs,
A flame ignites, and never dies.

Time weaves memories, soft and clear,
In every glance, you feel it near.
A cherished embrace through joys and tears,
This radiance grows through all the years.

Together they shine, a brilliant pair,
In love's embrace, beyond compare.
Cherished radiance, a bond so tight,
In every moment, pure delight.

The Beautiful Dance of Light

Across the sky, the colors play,
The beautiful dance of light each day.
Sunrise spills a golden hue,
A canvas bright, forever new.

In twilight's glow, the stars take flight,
A waltz of dreams in the velvet night.
With whispers soft, the moonlight glows,
A serenade the heart well knows.

Each flicker brings a secret shared,
In every shadow, love declared.
Together they swirl, in endless grace,
A timeless rhythm, a warm embrace.

The dance goes on as seasons change,
Through playful winds and skies so strange.
In laughter's echo, they find their way,
The beautiful dance that lights the day.

With every heartbeat, a step anew,
In love's grand ball, just me and you.
Together we twirl, through joy and strife,
In this beautiful dance, we find our life.

Luminous Connection

In the stillness of the night,
Whispers dance in soft delight.
Eyes meet in a gentle gaze,
Hearts entwined in silent praise.

Threads of light weave through the air,
Binding souls with tender care.
Every moment feels so bright,
As we bask in shared delight.

The glow of dreams begins to rise,
Painting hopes across the skies.
United in this sacred space,
Together, we find our place.

A radiant spark ignites the spark,
Guiding us through shadows dark.
In this dance of fate and chance,
We find solace in our romance.

Connection, like a river flows,
In its depths, pure love bestows.
With each heartbeat, spirits soar,
In luminous ties, we want more.

Warmth of Starlit Shadows

Beneath a blanket of deep night,
Stars awaken, casting light.
Shadows dance on whispered dreams,
Together, we unravel seams.

The universe sings soft and low,
In the dark, our spirits glow.
Hand in hand, we roam the path,
Finding joy in nature's math.

Each twinkle weaves another tale,
A gentle breeze, a lover's sail.
In the warmth of soft delight,
We embrace the starlit night.

Time stands still under cosmic skies,
In your gaze, my spirit flies.
Wrapped in shadows, hearts entwined,
In this cosmos, love defined.

Moments shared beneath the hue,
Starlit shadows, just us two.
As the world fades far away,
In this warmth, forever stay.

Embrace of Dawn's First Light

From slumber's grasp, the day awakes,
A golden glow, the morning makes.
Birds sing sweetly in the trees,
Dancing gently in the breeze.

The world ignites in hues so bright,
Nature breathes in pure delight.
In each ray, new hopes arise,
A promise made beneath the skies.

As shadows yield to warming beams,
We walk together, chasing dreams.
With your hand, I'll face the day,
In this embrace, we find our way.

The sun, a canvas, paints our fate,
With each touch, we communicate.
In the light, our souls ignite,
Together, we shine, holding tight.

With morning's kiss, the past unwinds,
In dawn's embrace, a love that binds.
Every moment, fresh and bright,
We bloom anew in morning light.

Glow of Heartfelt Encounters

In crowded rooms, our paths align,
A spark ignites—it feels divine.
Voices soft, like whispered dreams,
In this moment, nothing seems.

Each smile shared, a thread we weave,
In our eyes, the hearts believe.
Connections form in fleeting glances,
In this dance of sweet romances.

With every laugh, the world feels new,
Stories shared, just me and you.
In the glow of every touch,
We discover love means so much.

Moments gathered, like precious art,
Each encounter, a beat of heart.
In the twilight, voices blend,
In the glow, we find our friend.

Together, we explore the night,
Chasing dreams in pure delight.
In every heartbeat, time suspends,
In heartfelt encounters, love transcends.

www.ingramcontent.com/pod-product-compliance
Ingram Content Group UK Ltd.
Pitfield, Milton Keynes, MK11 3LW, UK
UKHW032217171224
452513UK00010B/472